the Count...
Coll...

Button Crafts

Holly
... will spend hours at the flea market picking through bushels of interesting buttons.

Kate
... likes adding old buttons to new clothes but sometimes has trouble buttoning up.

Mary Elizabeth
... loves making mini quilts from homespun and antique buttons.

10¢

BUTTONS

Pearly round heirlooms... big square tortoise-shell coat buttons... tiny pink baby buttons... alphabet letters and plastic doggy shapes... domes inlaid with rhinestones... simple black and white shirt buttons... there is just no end to the wide variety of buttons out there!

Whether you like the thrill of the hunt for one more extra-ordinary treasure for your button collection, or you have a soft heart for Great Aunt Elsie's button-filled basket, there are bunches of button craft ideas for you ⤳ many fun ways to put your button prizes to good use!

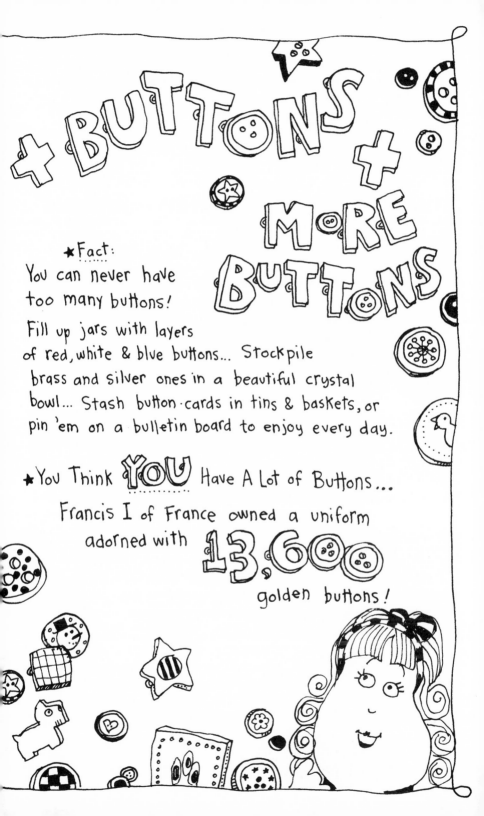

☆ BUTTONS ☆ MORE BUTTONS

★ Fact:
You can never have too many buttons!

Fill up jars with layers of red, white & blue buttons... Stockpile brass and silver ones in a beautiful crystal bowl... Stash button cards in tins & baskets, or pin 'em on a bulletin board to enjoy every day.

★ You Think YOU Have A Lot of Buttons...

Francis I of France owned a uniform adorned with 13,600 golden buttons!

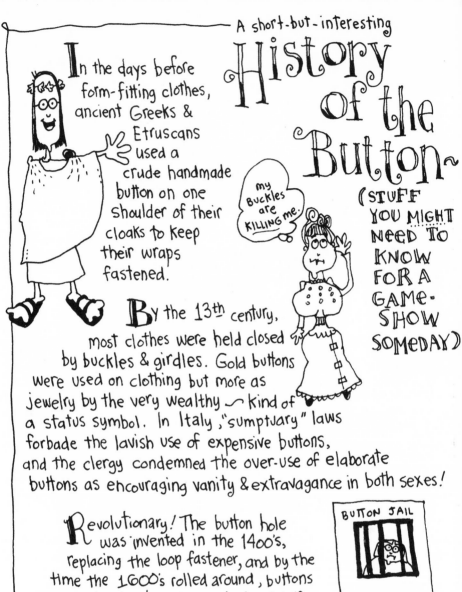

A short-but-interesting

History of the Button~

(STUFF YOU MIGHT NEED TO KNOW FOR A GAME-SHOW SOMEDAY)

In the days before form-fitting clothes, ancient Greeks & Etruscans used a crude handmade button on one shoulder of their cloaks to keep their wraps fastened.

my Buckles are KILLING me.

By the 13th century, most clothes were held closed by buckles & girdles. Gold buttons were used on clothing but more as jewelry by the very wealthy ~ kind of a status symbol. In Italy, "sumptuary" laws forbade the lavish use of expensive buttons, and the clergy condemned the over-use of elaborate buttons as encouraging vanity & extravagance in both sexes!

Revolutionary! The button hole was invented in the 1400's, replacing the loop fastener, and by the time the 1600's rolled around, buttons were used not only as a way to keep your pants up but as heirloom jewelry. Gold, silver, pearl, garnet & diamonds adorned elaborate buttons among the wealthy and were passed down as dowry. Less prosperous folk made do with pewter, brass, wood, bone & glass buttons.

BUTTON JAIL

CHECK OUT MY BUTTONS!

BEN

Most buttons were furnished by European factories until the 19th century. American buttons began to appear in New England, perhaps as early as 1706 ~ some experts believe Philadelphia was a hotbed for early button·makers!

During Victorian times, beautiful hand·painted buttons came into favor. Delicate enamel & glass, bejeweled & brass were sought·after buttons, and tiny portraits adorned some elegant versions.

BUTTONS

Buttons became more utilitarian during America's war years as raw materials became more scarce. Some manufacturers turned to ingenious methods for finding button materials ~ one bought up plastic windshields from obsolete bombers!

It is not I that belongs to the past, but the past that belongs to me. ~ Mary Antin

BUTTON MUSEUM

⑤

a New Face for an Old Vase

Treat your old vases and vintage bottles to a neat,
new facelift... glue on a bunch o' buttons!
Just imagine ~ red tulips in a clear milk
bottle decorated with bright crimson dots of color!
A cobalt blue vase with yellow buttons and filled
with yellow daisies! The possibilities are endless!

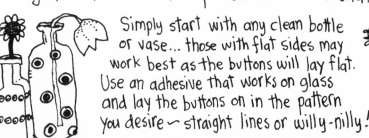

Simply start with any clean bottle
or vase... those with flat sides may
work best as the buttons will lay flat.
Use an adhesive that works on glass
and lay the buttons on in the pattern
you desire ~ straight lines or willy-nilly!

Buttons
and
Blossoms

… a colorful combination in a clear glass vase!

Pour a handful of plastic buttons in the bottom of the container, then add the flowers and water. Add more buttons if you like to hold the stems in place!

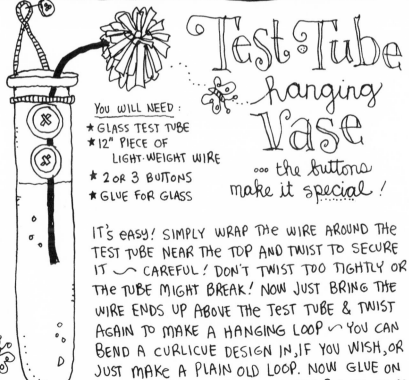

Test·Tube
hanging
Vase

ooo the buttons make it special!

YOU WILL NEED:
* GLASS TEST TUBE
* 12" PIECE OF LIGHT·WEIGHT WIRE
* 2 OR 3 BUTTONS
* GLUE FOR GLASS

IT'S EASY! SIMPLY WRAP THE WIRE AROUND THE TEST TUBE NEAR THE TOP AND TWIST TO SECURE IT ~ CAREFUL! DON'T TWIST TOO TIGHTLY OR THE TUBE MIGHT BREAK! NOW JUST BRING THE WIRE ENDS UP ABOVE THE TEST TUBE & TWIST AGAIN TO MAKE A HANGING LOOP ~ YOU CAN BEND A CURLICUE DESIGN IN, IF YOU WISH, OR JUST MAKE A PLAIN OLD LOOP. NOW GLUE ON A BUTTON OR 2 OR 3, ADD WATER & A BLOSSOM!

Button~Front Brag Book

~ a wonderful way to showcase precious photos <u>and</u> treasured buttons!

1. Start with a plain and simple photo album... maybe a pastel color for baby photos, or a nice brown kraft paper cover for old family pictures.

2. Make a color copy of a favorite photograph (use the color copier even for black-and-white photos to capture every shadow and nuance) and glue it to the cover of your photo album.

3. Find 5 beautiful buttons that coordinate with your project ~ maybe tiny white baby buttons for a baby album, or heirloom mother-of-pearl buttons to set off a family heritage themed brag book. Use your glue gun to attach one button to each of the 4 corners of your cover photo; take that 5th button and glue it on the right-hand side of the cover, about halfway down.

4. Wrap a pretty piece of thin ribbon or lace around the book and tie in a simple bow right where you glued on that last button... a nice finishing touch to your very personalized brag book!

Dress up a Diary!

A Dear Diary can be dressed up by attaching buttons on the cover in the shape of a heart or star!

Jazz up a Journal!

Encourage a kid to keep a journal by giving her a nifty notebook decorated with her name on the cover — use ALPHABET buttons from the fabric store.

Words form the thread on which we string our experiences. — ALDOUS HUXLEY

LOVE Friends Life

One-Button iDeas

Wrap a <u>wire hanger</u> with satin ribbon and tie the ends near the top where the wire "coils" together; Sew or hotglue a big button over the ribbon knot.

Use creamy-colored satin and a mother of pearl button for a beautiful christening dress hanger~ bright red ribbon and a gingham button for hanging a child's special dress!

Visit your local fabric store and give the <u>novelty</u> button rack a twirl! Use a pair of pliers to break off the little "sewing" loop from the button backs, and hotglue the buttons on pinbacks for colorful lapel pins. You can have a pin for every occasion!

Hang your favorite framed photos by a pretty braided cord on a button-topped nail. Just hot·glue 'em on for a quick way to dress your picture gallery!

BUTTON Memory BOARD

... give a hum-drum bulletin board **PIZAZZ!**

Simple! Buy a wooden-framed cork bulletin board and paint the frame a pretty color. Then hotglue a collection of buttons to the frame, all the way around! You may want to add other tiny trinkets to the button mix, too ∿ try charms, dimestore gems & old costume jewelry, marbles or teensy toys for a delightful look. (And don't forget to decorate your push pins ... no plain old thumb tacks for you! Glue favorite buttons on flat-top metal tacks for a fun way to pin up photos & ephemera!)

Handpaint a Button!

So simple yet so special! Begin with plain old wooden buttons... sand lightly and paint a background color — maybe pumpkin orange or snowman white. Add details with a very small paintbrush and acrylic paints, then lightly spray varnish to preserve your masterpiece!

In the late 1880s, young girls in the United States were crazy for "charm strings"... long chains of buttons collected one-by-one and sewn together.

1000 buttons was the goal girls reached for, since it was said Prince Charming would arrive after the 999th button was sewn on! Very few completed charm strings have been found.

Easy Ideas for Handpainted BUTTONS

..♥..

🌸 Add PATRIOTIC PUNCH to a shirt with FLAG buttons!

 Stripe a wooden button (square ones would be neat) with thin red & white lines. When dry, add a navy blue star.

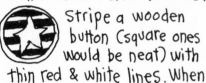 (KATE SAYS,"SKIP THE STRIPES AND JUST PAINT A FREE·HAND STAR RIGHT ON THE WOODEN BUTTON ⌣ IF IT'S CROOKED, SO WHAT ??")

🌸 Kids love to see their names in print ⌣ how about hand·painting letters on buttons to spell out a name? Sew 'em on a

 special sweater, or glue them on thumbtacks for the bulletin board.

🌸 Simple polkadots are easy to make and look oh-so-cute on a button or two.

Invitation Inspiration!

You know those teeny-tiny buttons that come on doll clothes and antique baby dresses? Can you think of anything so sweet? Sew one little button on a plain pink or blue foldover card for a darling baby shower invitation! Inside the card, hand·write this message with the party particulars:

♥

tiny buttons on little clothes
tiny socks for teensy toes
blankies, bears & lullaby tunes
a little baby's coming soon!

♥

THROW A BUTTON BASH!

Spend a chilly afternoon with your best buddies doing fun button crafts... snacking on yummy "food buttons"... while trading your real buttons!

Invite a handful of crafting friends over... Prepare one of the easy craft ideas from this book and have all the supplies on hand for your partiers to make one to take home ... maybe a country bookmark made of homespun or a set of hand-painted buttons to jazz up a denim shirt. Just have a good old time!

Button BASH Notions

Here's a thought: Ask your button buddies to bring a sewing notion to the party ~ thread, needles, thimbles, buttons, scissors. Put together a sewing basket for your local homeless shelter.

Have each friend bring 2 dozen buttons to the get-together. Throw them all in a pot for all the crafters to use, or have fun trading them.

If you have ooodles of extra buttons, fill a babyfood jar for each guest to take home as a party favor. Tie a scrap of homespun around the lid and hot glue on a button! Fun

Serve a button snack!
~ CHEESY ~
BUTTON BALL

1 · 8 oz. pkg. Neufchâtel cheese, softened
½ c. celery, finely chopped
⅓ c. Parmesan cheese, grated
¼ c. carrot, shredded
2 T. mayonnaise
2 T. dried minced onion
sweet red peppers & green onions to garnish

—

Mix all ingredients except for peppers & green onions in a medium bowl. On a platter, shape cheese mixture into a 1" high by 5" diameter circle. Cover & refrigerate overnight to allow flavors to blend. Garnish cheese circle with strips of red pepper and "dots" of green onion to resemble a button. Serve with round snack crackers.

Happiness is often the result of being too BUSY to be miserable. —ANONYMOUS

Sugar Cookie Buttons

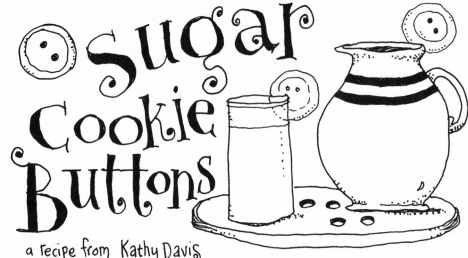

a recipe from Kathy Davis
* Presque Isle, ME

1·½ c. sugar
1·½ c. plus 3 T. butter, softened & divided
2 eggs
3 T. vanilla extract, divided
4 c. all-purpose flour
1 t. salt
1 t. baking soda
1 t. cream of tartar
1·½ c. powdered sugar
1 T. milk

In a mixing bowl, combine sugar & 1½ cups butter; beat 'til creamy. Add eggs & vanilla; beat well. Stir together flour, salt, baking soda & cream of tartar; gradually add to creamed mixture until completely blended. Chill for 30 minutes. On a lightly floured surface, roll dough to a ¼-inch thickness. Cut with a round cookie cutter dipped in flour. Using a spatula, transfer cookies to ungreased cookie sheets. Bake at 350° for 10 to 12 minutes. Cool on wire racks. For frosting, combine powdered sugar, remaining butter, vanilla & milk; beat until creamy. Thin with additional milk if necessary. Makes 7 dozen cookies.

16

BUTTON COOKIES à la HOLLY

Decorate your iced Sugar Cookie Buttons with "button holes" — strategically placed chocolate chips, red hots or any small, round cake-decoration-kind-of candy!

You might like to pipe on stripes for fancy button cookies, or add an initial in icing for fun party cookies!

Pack a cookie tin full of Buttons...edible ones, I mean! Hot glue bright & pretty buttons on the tin's lid — a delicious gift for a fellow button glutton.

Make one BIG old button cookie! Roll dough out to ¼ inch thickness and press it into a round foil cake pan. Bake to a golden brown, then when it's cool, ice with a colored frosting. Use licorice laces to make "thread" criss-crosses — sprinkle with edible glitter or colored sugar just for fun, and take your cookie to your next quilt guild meeting or crafting get-together.

All we need to make us really happy is something to be Enthusiastic about.

— CHARLES KINGSLEY —

Let's Play Dress Up!

Dress up our run-of-the-mill clothes with BUTTONS, that is! Sew on a few well-chosen buttons and you can change ordinary into spectacular!

SOME IDEAS

A plain old can always be improved upon! Any kind of hat, from a ballcap to a straw garden hat can benefit from a button or two. Try ducky-shaped buttons in yellow on a blue sunhat's brim... daisy-shaped buttons and red rick-rack on a gardener's shade hat!

Wooly mittens & gloves get all gussied up with buttons sewn around the edges. (And you don't have to be a little kid to enjoy silly mittens!)

A rhinestone button on black flats...bright purple buttons on white sneakers... red heart buttons on bedroom slippers ~ SHOE FUN!

String together a collection of buttons for an eye-catching bracelet or necklace.
Cut a piece of elastic string twice as long as your desired finished product (you can trim the excess string when you're done but you don't want to end up with not-enough-string!). Experiment with different layering methods when stringing the buttons to show off the pretty faces. Shiny metal heirloom button bracelets are beautiful and dressy ⌒ colorful plastic buttons on a string are merry additions to casual clothes!

Sew a row of little buttons around the hem of a long skirt or jumper for a custom look.

Common denim shirts turn ZINGY with gingham buttons! And all the buttons don't need to match··· use a ZIPPY combination of colors just for fun.

Button Up! Basic straw purses & tote bags get the special treatment with the addition of pretty tortoiseshell or brass buttons.

Button Up A PATRIOTIC POT

You Will Need:

* A CLEAN CLAY POT, any size
* PRE-MIXED WHITE GROUT
* A SPATULA
* VARIETY OF PATRIOTIC-COLORED BUTTONS — NAVY & WHITE ROUND BUTTONS, RED STAR-SHAPED BUTTONS — TOTAL OF 50 or 60 PIECES

Okay, here's what you do! Grab hold of the clay pot and dig your spatula into the grout — get a pretty good size glob and apply to the pot. Pretend you're "buttering" the pot, and put the grout on just about the depth of your buttons. Be sure to cover the whole pot exterior—no bare or thin spots! (You may want to put on rubber gloves and pat the grout with your fingers to smooth it out.) Now here's the fun part — start sticking the buttons into the wet grout! When buttons are set (maybe 5 minutes or so), take a wet paper towel and gently clean off extra grout that's on top of the buttons. Allow to dry overnight.

GROUT

Other Button Pot Thoughts

◉ Use alphabet letter buttons and bright round shirt buttons to spell out a <u>name</u> on a pot for a fun gift.

◎ <u>Holiday</u> pots are inexpensive to make and great decorations! Try red & green buttons on a pot with tree-shaped buttons with little pines planted inside for Christmas; black & orange buttons for a Halloween pot, pink & yellow for Easter pots!

Thank You, Mrs. Patterson!

Over the years, countless women have saved buttons that were too pretty to toss out with worn-out clothing...

One of those homemakers is credited with being the first full-fledged button collector. In the 1930s, Mrs. Gertrude Patterson gave a radio talk on collecting, and spurred a Depression-era craze. Button collecting was inexpensive, practical and easily accessible!

KID • FRIENDLY

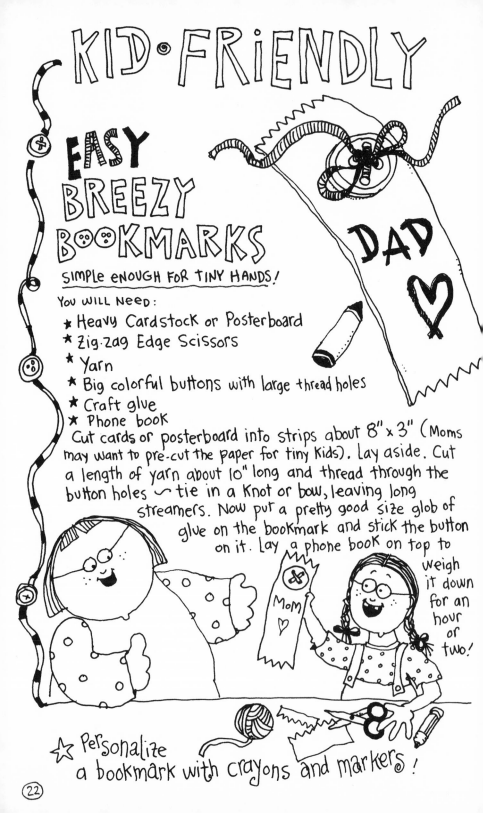

EASY BREEZY BOOKMARKS

SIMPLE ENOUGH FOR TINY HANDS!

YOU WILL NEED:

* Heavy Cardstock or Posterboard
* Zig-zag Edge Scissors
* Yarn
* Big colorful buttons with large thread holes
* Craft glue
* Phone book

Cut cards or posterboard into strips about 8" x 3" (Moms may want to pre-cut the paper for tiny kids). Lay aside. Cut a length of yarn about 10" long and thread through the button holes — tie in a knot or bow, leaving long streamers. Now put a pretty good size glob of glue on the bookmark and stick the button on it. Lay a phone book on top to weigh it down for an hour or two!

DAD ♡

MOM ♡

☆ Personalize a bookmark with crayons and markers!

BUTTON CRAFTS

CREEPY BUTTON BUGS

ORNERY LITTLE BOYS & GIRLS LOVE 'EM!

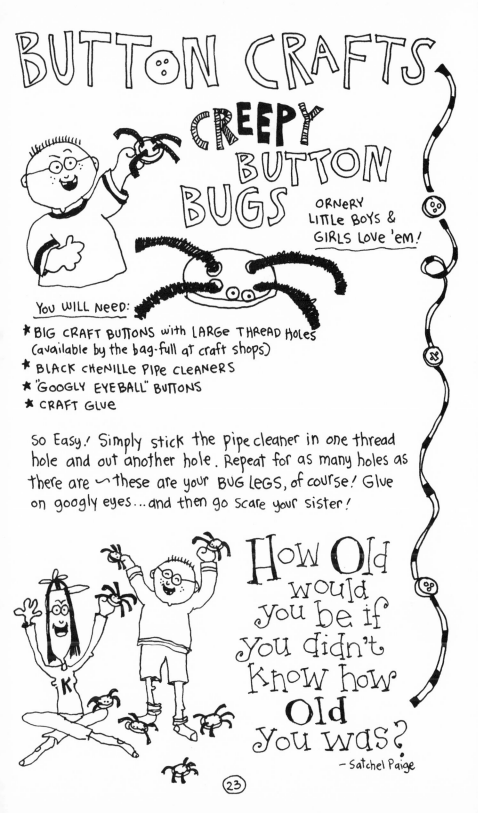

YOU WILL NEED:

* BIG CRAFT BUTTONS with LARGE THREAD HOLES (available by the bag-full at craft shops)
* BLACK CHENILLE PIPE CLEANERS
* "GOOGLY EYEBALL" BUTTONS
* CRAFT GLUE

So Easy! Simply stick the pipe cleaner in one thread hole and out another hole. Repeat for as many holes as there are ⌐ these are your BUG LEGS, of course! Glue on googly eyes...and then go scare your sister!

How Old would you be if you didn't Know how Old you was?

— Satchel Paige

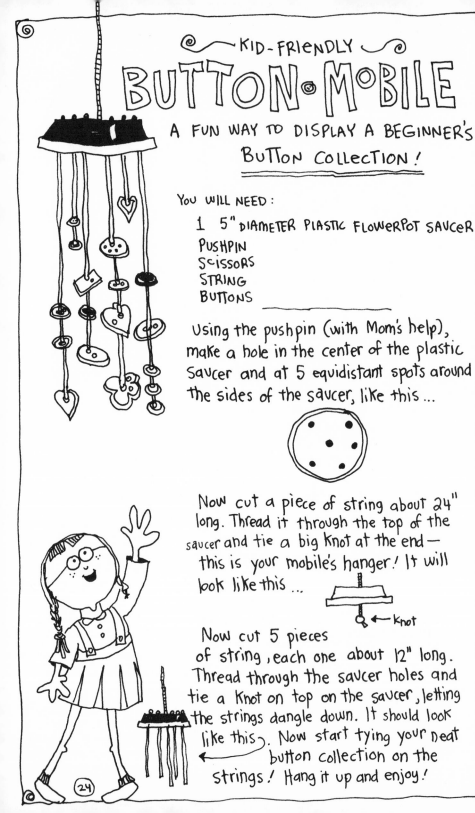

KID-FRIENDLY BUTTON MOBILE

A FUN WAY TO DISPLAY A BEGINNER'S BUTTON COLLECTION!

YOU WILL NEED:

1 5" DIAMETER PLASTIC FLOWERPOT SAUCER
PUSHPIN
SCISSORS
STRING
BUTTONS

Using the pushpin (with Mom's help), make a hole in the center of the plastic saucer and at 5 equidistant spots around the sides of the saucer, like this...

Now cut a piece of string about 24" long. Thread it through the top of the saucer and tie a big knot at the end — this is your mobile's hanger! It will look like this...

← knot

Now cut 5 pieces of string, each one about 12" long. Thread through the saucer holes and tie a knot on top on the saucer, letting the strings dangle down. It should look like this. Now start tying your neat button collection on the strings! Hang it up and enjoy!

WHAT·DO·YOU·MEAN I'M·KINDA·OLD FOR·THESE·CRAFT·IDEAS?

NeveR ★TOO★ OLD
Button Crafts
(FOR KIDS of ALL AGes)

whimsical, wonderful **BUTTON WORMS**
can be fashioned by threading
buttons on a fuzzy pipe cleaner! Pack 'em on
pretty tight and add some curly antennae on
the front... and don't forget to glue on 2 googly eyeballs!

SEE? I TOLD YOU I WASN'T TOO OLD.

Hey! WHAT's cheerier than a paper
party hat? Why, a **BUTTONED-
UP PARTY HAT**, of course! Just
glue on a handful of bright plastic
buttons all over the hat — fun, fun, fun!

You'RE RIGHT!

(This works on a **PAPER CROWN**, too — buttons
are almost as good as diamonds & rubies.)

GOOD PLACES TO GO ON A BUTTON HUNT

☆ Granny's Button Basket ☆ Garage Sales ☆ Flea
Markets & Antique Shops (look in little dishes full of junk,
jewelry boxes & baskets of lace & trims) ☆ Second·Hand Clothing
Stores (check out the old shirts & skirts for button treasures)
☆ The Internet ☆ The National Button Society (check your library
for address) ☆ Local Button Clubs ☆ Friends!

㉕

A BLOOMIN' BUTTON AUTOGRAPH PILLOW

How much fun is <u>this</u>? Find a plain canvas or cotton pillow, whatever size you like... a bright color is good.

Buy a big old silk daisy at the craft store and take off the stem — all you need is the flower head. Use your trusty glue gun to attach a vivid button in the middle of the blossom — make the button a big one for visual PUNCH! — then glue the blossom smack in the middle of the pillow. Use a fabric pen to sign up!

Holly
Jackie
KATE
JoAnn

BUTTON Pillow variations

Make an autograph pillow for a kid's slumber party using a cotton pillowcase:

molly

Glue the flower heads on the pillowcase near the pillow opening... and don't forget the buttons!

Have your pillowcase **monogrammed** with the word "FRIENDS" or with a name before you attach your button flower heads... a great gift for a going-away friend. Everybody can sew on a special button and add a signature in fabric pen.

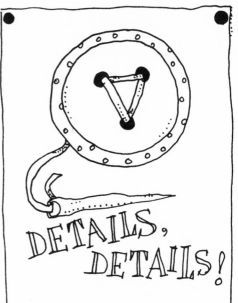

DETAILS, DETAILS!

When you're making button crafts, you may want to experiment using the buttons **with and without** thread in the holes. Please your eye ⌇ does it look better to have a snazzy shot of colored thread running through the design, or does the beauty of the button stand alone?

Beauty is in the eye of the beholder.
—OLD SAYING

FOR THE BUTTON·HAPPY·BUT·THREAD·IMPAIRE

NO-SEW IDEAS

★ Plain old curtains get a jolly look when you glue on a row of vibrant buttons! Dress up a valance or panels by attaching buttons on the hem with fabric glue or your trusty old glue gun. Try navy buttons on red gingham kitchen curtains ∽ sweet!

★ Same idea: light up a sad old lampshade with a handful of colorful buttons. Just hotglue them on around the edge... and if you get carried away, go ahead and trim a ceramic lamp base with buttons, too! Put the buttons on in a nice, neat row or go for a polka-dot effect!

★ Cover the back of a plastic hand-mirror with bunches of buttons! Hot glue them on one-by one, starting in the middle of the mirror's back ∽ a charming gift for your favorite button collector.

Isn't it splendid to think of all the things there are to find out about? It just makes me glad to be alive — it's such an interesting world.

~ LUCY MONTGOMERY

28

more button ideas

Glue a unique button on a teeny square of magnet for instant and interesting *Refrigerator Magnets.* Make a whole bunch!

Make a basketful of *Button Balls!* Simply spray paint a Styrofoam ball your choice of any country color. When it's dry, get out your glue gun and start attaching button after button after button. It's a pretty way to showcase buttons you've collected!

Determine never to be idle... it is wonderful how much may be done if we are always doing. —THOMAS JEFFERSON

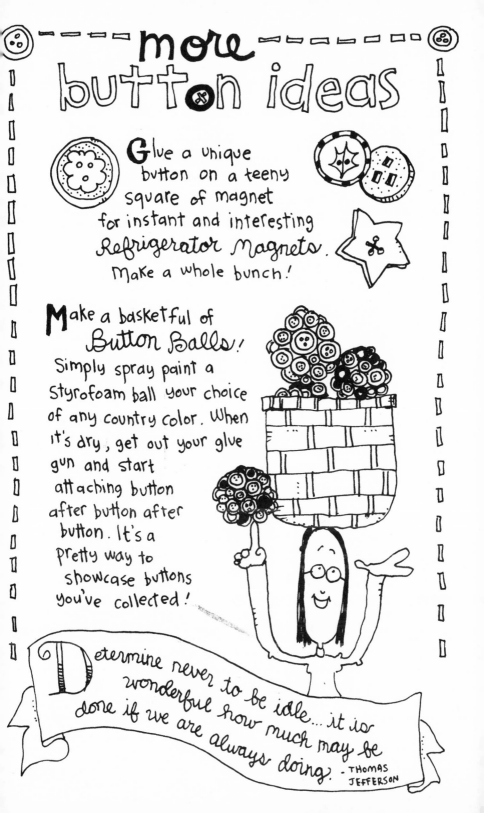

GLUE-GUN MAGIC!

—DECORATED—
BUTTON FRAMES
So many photos, so many ideas!

◎ A PLAIN WHITE FRAME DECORATED WITH IVORY BUTTONS LOOKS BEAUTIFUL AROUND A WEDDING PHOTO. ASK AT THE WEDDING DRESS SHOP IF YOU CAN BUY A BUTTON OR TWO LIKE THOSE USED ON THE BRIDE'S DRESS FOR A PERSONAL TOUCH!

◎ GLUE ON A GINGHAM BOW and A TEENY PASTEL BUTTON FOR A GREAT BABY FRAME IDEA. YOU MIGHT EVEN MAKE A LONG RIBBON LOOP AT THE FRAME'S TOP FOR WALL-HANGING.

◎ A DARK WOOD FRAME GETS A YEE-HAW DRESS-UP WITH SILVER STAR OR HAMMERED-SILVER BUTTONS!

◎ THREE CHEERS FOR YOUR FAVORITE SCHOOL COLORS: GLUE SCHOOL-COLORED BUTTONS ALL AROUND A FRAME FOR A GOOD GIFT FOR A GOING-AWAY-TO-COLLEGE KID... DON'T FORGET TO MAKE ONE FOR THE EMPTY-NEST MOM & DAD, TOO!

◎ NOVELTY BONE & DOGGY-SHAPED BUTTONS FROM THE CRAFT SHOP ARE CUTE ADD-ONS TO A FRAME FOR SPOTTY'S PICTURE.

Check out the HUGE variety of buttons at your local fabric/craft store - you'll be AMAZED!

★ In the early 1900s, china buttons were decorated with calico prints for puritanical sections of American society that preferred "invisible" buttons.

Button Up a Gift!

Heavy-weight paper hang tags from the office supply store get a new look with a bright button! Just glue on one or a handful and tie on a pretty ribbon for a great gift tag.

Wrap a box in plain white paper and fold a wide piece of shiny red satin ribbon around it. Plop a large white button on top ⌣ lovely & simple! (Kraft paper & brown buttons look country terrific, too, with raffia ribbon)

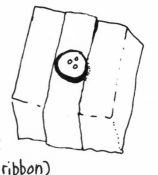

are Those ALL for me?

Fancy-up an everyday brown paper lunch bag! Use pinking shears or decorative-edged scissors on the open end of the bag... put a gift inside and fold the top over. With a needle and thread, sew a big button right over the folded edge to keep the bag shut. Leave thread ends long for visual ooomph!

Just Imagine

A rock pile ceases to be a rock pile the moment a single man contemplates it, bearing within him the image of a cathedral

- Antoine de Saint-Exupery -